KIDDING AROUND

CHICAGO

A YOUNG PERSON'S GUIDE TO THE CITY

LAUREN DAVIS

ILLUSTRATED BY SALLY BLAKEMORE

John Muir Publications
Santa Fe, New Mexico

*For Aaron and Peter Lazar,
A.B. Willson, B.B. Coll,
C. and D. Hall.*

*Special thanks to Jamie and
Stuart Abelson, Jan and Don
Barliant, Peter Gambaccini,
Larry Hildes, Daktahmo
Nelligan, Andrew Patner,
and Marion Rosenbluth*

*Buckingham Fountain is
280 feet across at the bot-
tom, spouts water 135
feet into the air, and con-
tains 1,500,000 gallons of
water.*

John Muir Publications, P.O. Box 613, Santa Fe, NM 87504

© 1990 by Lauren Davis
Illustrations © 1990 by Sally Blakemore
Cover © 1990 by John Muir Publications
All rights reserved. Published 1990
Printed in the United States of America

Library of Congress Cataloging-in-Publication Data
Davis, Lauren, 1955-
    Kidding around Chicago : a young person's guide to the
city / Lauren Davis; illustrated by Sally Blakemore.
        p.   cm.
    Summary: Provides historical and cultural information
as well as a guide to the sights of Chicago and its suburbs.
    ISBN 0-945465-70-X
    1. Chicago (Ill.)—Description—1981- —Guide-books—
Juvenile literature. 2. Children—Travel—Illinois—
Chicago—Guide-books—Juvenile literature. [1. Chicago
(Ill.)—Description—Guides.]
I. Blakemore, Sally, ill. II. Title.
F548.18.D38   1990
917.73'110443—dc20   90-6494
                                                              CIP
                                                               AC

Designer: Joanna Hill
Typeface: Trump Medieval
Typesetter: Copygraphics, Santa Fe, New Mexico
Printer: Guynes Printing Company of New Mexico

Distributed to the book trade by:
W. W. Norton & Company, Inc.
New York, New York

Contents

Wow... Today was Awesome!

To remember everything you see, hear, feel, and taste while traveling, bring along a journal. Write in it. Draw pictures. Press flowers between the pages. Take along a tape recorder. Talk into it and interview the people you meet.

1. Why the Windy City? / 4

2. Windy City Time Line / 8

3. River, Bird's-eye, Lakefront, and Elevated Views / 10

4. Succulents, Simians, and Sea Lions (Lincoln Park/Depaul) / 16

5. Cows and Rock 'n Roll (Near North, North Pier, River North) / 24

6. The Loop: Pork Bellies, Cattle, and Calder (Downtown) / 31

7. More Loop / 36

8. Mummies, Mollies, and Moon Rocks (South of the Loop) / 41

9. Science, Sojourner, and the South Side / 45

10. Fortune Cookies and Fried Eel (Ethnic Neighborhoods) / 49

11. The Outer Limits (Chicago Suburbs) / 55

12. Wave Good-bye to the Windy City / 57

Events in the Windy City / 58

Appendix / 61

1. Why the Windy City?

Why do people call the most magnificent midwestern metropolis—home of the world's tallest building, delectable deep dish pizza, and the Chicago Cubs—the "Windy City"?

Rumor has it that the wind in the Windy City is strong enough to knock folks off the sidewalks. While it's true that when an easterly "Hawk" kicks up you'll grab your hat and the nearest lamppost, Chicago does not get its nickname from stormy weather. The nickname comes from a New York reporter who claimed Chicagoans were full of "wind" because they bragged so about their city's attributes while they were bidding to become hosts for the 1893 World's Fair. The name stuck. Residents and outsiders alike began referring to Chicago as the "Windy City."

Chicagoans still love to boast about the city's beginnings when it was a marshy, smelly swampland called *che-cau-gua* (which means something like "great," "wild onion," or "skunk cabbage," depending on who you talk to) by the area's earliest residents, Native Americans.

The first non-Indian settlers in the area were French explorers and fur trappers who arrived in

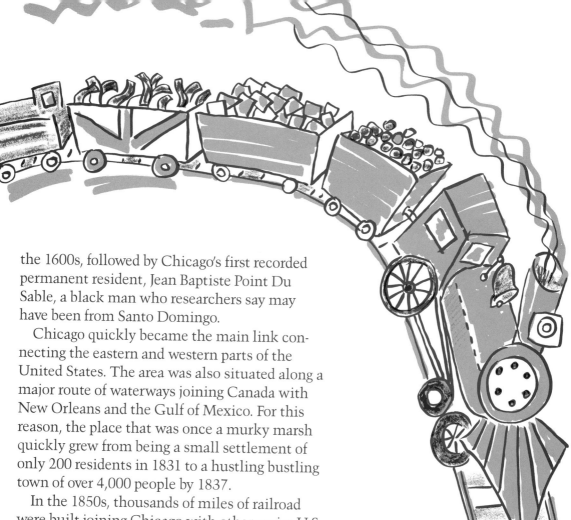

the 1600s, followed by Chicago's first recorded permanent resident, Jean Baptiste Point Du Sable, a black man who researchers say may have been from Santo Domingo.

Chicago quickly became the main link connecting the eastern and western parts of the United States. The area was also situated along a major route of waterways joining Canada with New Orleans and the Gulf of Mexico. For this reason, the place that was once a murky marsh quickly grew from being a small settlement of only 200 residents in 1831 to a hustling bustling town of over 4,000 people by 1837.

In the 1850s, thousands of miles of railroad were built joining Chicago with other major U.S. cities. The Windy City soon became the central hub of shipping and trade for the entire nation. People came from all over the country to work on the expanding railways. They also came from around the globe—from Germany, Ireland, Sweden, Eastern Europe, Italy, Greece, and Africa—to find opportunity. The city, now with a population of over 3 million, has more recently become home to Arab, Mexican, Chinese, Vietnamese, West African, and East Indian immigrants,

"Hawk" refers to the cold slicing wind that whips out of the Chicago winter sky. The term became popular after Chicago rhythm and blues singer Lou Rawls sang about the hawk in his song "Dead End Street."

Chicago is often called the "Second City" because it was once second in size after New York, but it has actually been surpassed in population by Los Angeles.

many of whom have settled in the Windy City's ethnic neighborhoods. This mix of language and culture makes the city a place Chicagoans are proud of.

Walk through a few of Chicago's neighborhoods, and in the markets you'll see barrels of East Indian spices, wiggly octopuses, silk saris, and live crabs. You'll smell tortillas baking and hear people speaking the languages of their native countries.

The CTA (Chicago Transit Authority) provides an efficient, cheap way to get around. Children under 7 ride the buses, subways, and elevated lines for free. If you're between 7 and 11, public transportation costs 50 cents. In warm weather, walking, riding bikes, roller skating, and even skateboarding are great ways to get around.

If you plan to visit the Windy City in winter, remember it really is windy! And cold! But if you bundle up, this great city, which sits by Lake Michigan and is straddled by the Chicago River (both its branches), is a winter wonderland of fun. Whatever the weather, Chicago can be your kind of town.

So, if you're ready for Chicago-style hot dogs, views from the top of the world, baseball, basketball, pork bellies, pyramids, parks, Picasso, mummies, sea mammals, submarines, space shuttles, zoo animals, the stars and the heavens above, jazz, blues, theater, symphonies, sculpture, skiing, skating, kite flying, souvenir buying, gangsters, and just about anything else you can think of, grab your copy of *Kidding Around Chicago* and get ready for one of the windiest cities of all, a city that's second to none, Frank Sinatra's "kind of town" and soon to be yours, too—Chicago!

When in the Windy City, remember that **Lake Michigan is always east.** The City follows a simple grid system with **Madison and State streets** at the baseline. The street numbers get higher the farther away in any direction you travel from Madison and State. The northern and southern parts of the city are divided by **Madison. State Street** separates eastern streets from western streets. You can't get lost in Chicago if you're traveling west or north. Every multiple of 800 represents a mile. So, for example if you are at 800 N. Michigan you are one mile north of the baseline.

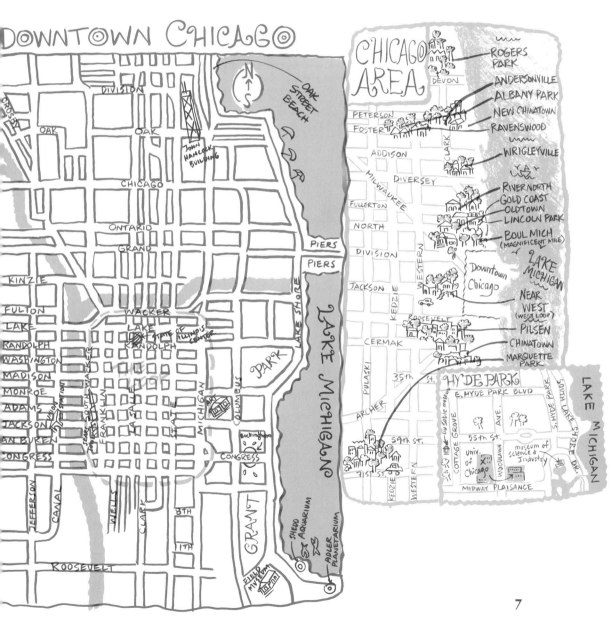

2. Windy City Time Line

1600—Before this date, Chicago was inhabited by the Illinois, Miami, Wea, and Potawatomi Indians.

1673—Pere Jacques Marquette and Louis Jolliet explore Chicago.

1779—Jean Baptiste Point Du Sable, Chicago's first permanent resident, builds his home near the banks of the Chicago River.

1804—Fort Dearborn is built to protect white settlers from Native Americans who are struggling to regain the area.

1806—By this time, Chicago is recognized as an important crossroads.

1812—Fort Dearborn is abandoned by the military. There is much fighting between whites and Native Americans.

1816—Fur trappers and traders and military personnel return to Fort Dearborn.

1832—Black Hawk, Chief of the Sac and Fox Indians, is defeated and forced to sign a treaty stating he will remain west of the Chicago River.

1833—Chicago has 300 residents and is officially incorporated.

1834—The first professional paid entertainment includes an exhibition of ventriloquism and fire eating. Admission: 25 cents.

1840—The Chicago Anti-Slavery Society holds its first public meeting.

1857—There are now 4,000 miles of railroad tracks connecting Chicago with other major U.S. cities.

1860—Abraham Lincoln, native of Illinois, is elected president of the United States.

1865—The Chicago Stockyards are opened.

1871—Mrs. O'Leary's cow kicks over a lantern, causing a fire that burns the entire town. Ninety thousand people are left homeless.

1870s—Famous architects begin to rebuild Chicago.

1894—Black and white railway workers strike to protest low wages.

1900—Chicago Sanitary and Ship Canal is completed to permanently and efficiently reverse flow of Chicago River.

1919—Gangster Al Capone, responsible for the 1929 St. Valentine's Day Massacre, comes to town.

1934—Gangster John Dillinger is killed at the Biograph movie theater by FBI agents.

1942—Scientists at the University of Chicago split the atom in a secret laboratory underneath the stands at Stagg Field.

1955—Richard J. Daley, one of the most famous mayors in U.S. history, is elected.

1968—The Democratic National Convention is held in Chicago and thousands of people protesting against the unpopular Vietnam War are beaten by police and National Guardsmen.

1975—Construction is completed on Sears Tower, the world's tallest skyscraper.

1983—Chicago's first black mayor, Harold Washington, is elected.

1985—State of Illinois Center Building opens.

3. River, Bird's-eye, Lakefront, and Elevated Views

The best way to find your bearings in the Windy City is to view it from several angles—from the great **Chicago River** and **Lake Michigan**, from along miles of beachfront at Chicago's eastern edge, from a thousand feet above the city in the observation deck of **Sears Tower**, and from the hair-raising roller coaster, **Ravenswood Elevated Subway Line**.

If you cross the river at Michigan Avenue and walk toward downtown, you will cross the **Michigan Avenue Bridge**, one of Chicago's 50 or so drawbridges. At any moment the bridge might be raised to give passage to a ship on its way upriver. (Don't worry about walking over bridges. Pedestrian and motor traffic is always cleared before bridges go up.)

The river used to flow into Lake Michigan until 1836, when Chicagoans built a temporary canal (the **Illinois-Michigan Canal**) that, through the force of gravity, caused the sluggish Chicago River to reverse its course. In 1900, the **Sanitary and Ship Canal** was built. The new permanent canal kept the water flowing from the lake into the river. This was done to keep the city's waste from polluting the lake, Chicago's

you rang?

Chicago, like all big cities, can be dangerous. Always travel with an adult, and if you get lost, stop a policeman or call 911 and someone will help you.

main source of drinking water. The Windy City's drinking water is now considered the cleanest of any urban area.

Chicagoans use the lake to play in as well as to drink from. To get a real feel of the city from the lake and the river, pack a p.b. & j. and hop on a **Wendella Sightseeing Boat** (Wendella's offices are in the Wrigley Building). Check out the skyline as the boat winds up and down the river and onto Lake Michigan.

Or cruise over to the south side of Michigan Avenue at the **Mercury Dock** and steal your way onto a **Wacky Pirate Cruise**. The buccaneers on board will give you a kazoo, tell you haunting tales of high seas, and spin a yarn or two about pirates who sailed Lake Michigan.

When you are back on dry land again, walk along Wacker Drive and look north across the bridge. Now you have a great view of the **Wrigley Building**, corporate headquarters of Wrigley chewing gum. Slightly east of the Wrigley Building and west of the **Equitable Building** is where some historians believe Chicago's first recorded resident, Jean Baptiste Point Du Sable, built his home sometime around 1779. Du Sable, of African and French descent, made his home on the banks of the Chicago River with his Native American wife.

As you walk west along the river, you will come to the original site of **Fort Dearborn** on N. Michigan and Wacker, built by white men to protect new settlers and this major crossroads of commerce from the area's original settlers, the Potawatomi Indians.

But the fort didn't help them for long. On August 15, 1812, the Potawatomi attacked Fort Dearborn. Many were killed, and the fort commander's wife was captured. She was bought back for the price of one mule and ten bottles of whiskey. The Potawatomi eventually lost all hold on the area, and, as you can see, the brass plaques in the sidewalk are the only reminder of the fort and those earlier days.

Farther west at **Wolf Point**, right across the **Franklin-Orleans Bridge**, is where the branches of the Chicago River meet. While there are no historic markers, and no one is quite sure where the name Wolf Point comes from, there are many stories floating around the city that this was the site of a trading post in 1778 and later the site of a rough-and-tumble tavern called the Rat Castle. Seeing the sky lined with towering skyscrapers,

The folks at Wrigley say Americans chew just under 300 sticks of gum per person, each year.

it's hard to imagine Chicago's wild frontier times.

The tallest building of all in Chicago is the 1,454-foot (1,707 feet if you include the two white antennas on top of the building) **Sears Tower** at N. Wacker and Adams.

It's not your imagination, that is the wind you hear howling as you step into the Sears Tower elevators that soar 1,353 feet in 55 seconds, carrying you up to the 103rd-floor **Skydeck Observatory**. You won't be able to feel it, but the 110-story building actually sways during strong winds. Don't worry, engineers built it that way to withstand the stormiest weather. So unless you feel uneasy about towering over the rest of the world, take a trip to the top and get a bird's-eye view of Chicago.

As you peer out of the bronze tinted windows, you can see the John Hancock Center to the north, the Adler Planetarium and the expanse of Lake Michigan to the east, and Comiskey Park, home of the Chicago White Sox (until sometime in 1991 when the ball park will be torn down and a new one will be built in its place), to the south. As you look west, you will see how quickly the tall cityscape gives way to smaller neighborhood buildings.

Unless you're interested in miles of mist, don't waste time or money going up to the Observatory when there is zero visibility. (Zero visibility means you can't see a thing.)

Hop into your hightops and walk, ride bikes, roller skate, or skateboard along part of Chicago's 29 miles of beachfront. You can get bike trail maps from Chicago's Bureau of Traffic Engineering and Operations on N. Clark Street. Most bicycle rental shops in the city do not specifi-

*Kids at **Francis Parker School** discovered Chicagoans will produce 2.5 million tons of garbage by 1991. The city's landfills will be full and the garbage will have no place to go. Even while traveling, you can recycle.*

13

The city began to develop the lakefront as a recreational area in the 1930s. Prior to this, the area consisted of miles of mucky muddy marshland. An Illinois state law declares the lakefront shall remain forever "open, clear, and free" so everyone can enjoy it.

cally rent kids' bikes, but you may find a bike that is right for you at **Bicycles Chicago Rental** on W. Randolph. In warm weather, you can rent bikes in Lincoln Park.

You can find roller skates at **United Skates of America** on N. Clark and cruise the lakefront beaches. These sandy shores aren't like California beaches, but sand combined with long stretches of concrete walkways and rusted piers are Chicago's version of beaches and Chicagoans are proud of them.

There are many underground passageways that will allow you to avoid having to cross traffic-laden Lake Shore Drive. These passageways take you right out to the water's edge. During summer months, don't forget to bring your fishing pole out to the beach. Lake Michigan is full of perch and coho salmon.

Another way to be on the edge of the city is to

catch the Ravenswood "EL" or ("L") subway line from the **Quincy/Wells/Loop L station**. Take this train around the loop to a neighborhood called **Albany Park**, where you can get out, wander around a bit, and have a bite of curried chicken with coconut milk at the **Thai Little Home Cafe** on Kedzie Avenue. But if this roller coaster "L" of a ride has you holding onto your hat and your stomach, you may want to wait until you get back to the Quincy/Wells station to have a slice of pizza at **Giordano's** on Wabash and Jackson.

As the train heads back into the city, you will get a great view of some of Chicago's many ethnic neighborhoods as well as a dramatic view of the city's skyline from the northwest.

Now you're ready to do some more exploring, touring, eating, shopping, and even some space

The renovated Quincy/Wells/Loop L station used to be heated by a potbelly stove. Before you step onto the train, look up at the ceilings. The molded tin looks the way it did in 1897.

4. Succulents, Simians, and Sea Lions (Lincoln Park / Depaul)

Save a bird: make a falcon silhouette for your window to protect small birds from flying into the glass. Lincoln Park Zoo Review *reminds you: don't wear belts, shoes, or coats made from endangered species.*

incoln Park, on Chicago's north side, is the city's largest park. Situated on 12,000 acres, it has 12 beaches, several museums, and a zoo with over 2,000 birds, mammals, and reptiles. It was used as a cemetery from 1810 to 1842. When the city decided to make it a park, thousands of bodies were moved to the city's other cemeteries. There may still be people buried there. As recently as the early 1980s, workmen widening the road discovered skeletons from several unmarked graves.

You won't find human skeletons in the **Chicago Historical Society**, but you can get a hands-on feel for some of Chicago's well-preserved historical events.

Touch beaver, badger, or muskrat skins, like ones used by the Potawatomi and fur traders as a way of barter. How many beaver skins would you pay to buy a cast iron skillet or a wool blanket?

In the **Pioneer Life Gallery**, you can see very authentic-looking pioneer women as they dip candles and weave on a loom built in the early 1800s.

Produce your own old-time radio show in the **Hands-on History Exhibit** using blocks of wood to create the sound of a gunshot or sheets of metal to make the sound of thunder, and then climb aboard the engine of the **Pioneer**, the first train to come through the city of Chicago in 1848.

As you leave the museum and head north, you will see a big red barn. That's right, it's a farm right in the middle of the city, known as the **Farm-in-the-Zoo**. The farm has several different barns with horses, cows, pigs, and chickens. In the Dairy Barn, you'll see how the butter you eat gets from cow to kitchen table. To watch the farm animals being fed, visit the barns around 9:00 a.m. or at about 3:00 p.m.

After watching the animals eat their dinners, you might be pretty hungry yourself, so head to the recently reopened **Cafe Brauer**, where hamburgers and hot dogs are served year-round. If you're not starving, wait and grab a Chicago-style hot dog at **Gold Coast Dogs** on the corner of N. Clark and W. Dickens.

If you still need to work up an appetite, you can rent pedal boats and pedal your way around **South Pond** or take a 30-minute walk around the pond's perimeter. You might see some wood ducks, mallards, and a fish or two.

But head on to the Sea Lion Pool at the **Lincoln Park Zoo** to see some real swimming. Even in the dead of winter, the seals and sea lions seem to be sunning themselves as if they were vacationing at a seaside resort.

You'll go ape at the Great Ape House, which houses the largest collection of apes in captivity in the entire world. It's downright eerie to watch gorillas with names like Debbie and Frank as they watch you watching them. Don't stare too

A Chicago-style hot dog isn't considered Chicago style without a fresh poppy seed bun, yellow mustard, hot short peppers, relish, and plenty of chopped onions. You may want to add tomato slices but never ketchup!

Experts estimate Chicagoans eat close to 24,000,000 hot dogs a year! Laid end to end, those hot dogs would stretch from Chicago to Los Angeles and maybe even a bit farther!

HOT DOG EXPERTS

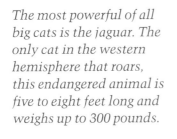

The most powerful of all big cats is the jaguar. The only cat in the western hemisphere that roars, this endangered animal is five to eight feet long and weighs up to 300 pounds.

much or they might start pounding on the glass. Gorillas, like all animals, need peace and quiet. So, please, be respectful when visiting the zoo.

To get a feel for some feline feelings, visit the endangered cats like snow leopards, cheetahs, and Siberian tigers at the new Kovler Lion House.

In 1989, more than 200 mammals, reptiles, and birds were born or hatched at the zoo. Many of these animals are considered to be threatened, endangered, or critically endangered species. To learn how Lincoln Park Zoo is working to help save the world's animals, become a member of the zoo and read the ***Zoo Review***, which lists current and upcoming workshops and events for children at the **Crown-Field Center** and at the Children's Zoo.

At the **Lincoln Park Children's Zoo** (considered the first children's zoo in the country to be open year-round), you can see baby animals like Kiri, the chimp, born in October 1989. He'll remind you of your kid brother as he sucks his thumb and stumbles around in his diapers. If you are careful and gentle, you might get a chance to pet goats and guinea pigs and maybe even an armadillo. It all depends on how the animals are feeling. Zoo officials explain that animals get stressed out just like people do and sometimes need to be left alone.

If *you're* stressed out and need to get away from the crowds that frequent the zoo (the world's busiest), take a break and walk to the **Lincoln Park Conservatory** and stroll through a jungle of exotic plants. This gigantic greenhouse features a 50-foot rubber tree from Africa and all kinds of weird exotic tropical plants from India, Brazil, and China.

Want to see a blue-winged teal, a gadwall, an American wigeon (not pigeon), or a greeb? Stop by the **Zoo Rookery**, reopening in fall 1990, and hang out with some of the zoo's flightier creatures.

The birds at the **Chicago Academy of Sciences** can't fly; as a matter of fact, most of the animals here don't move at all because they're stuffed! The Academy, just west of Cafe Brauer and across Stockton Drive, has a stuffed moose, bears, birds, wolves, and models of prehistoric fish. A recently opened exhibit called "Prehistoric Sea Monsters: Dinosaurs and the Deep" featured giant robotic prehistoric creatures in a simulated underwater environment.

For a closer look at how to solve some of the

Seals and sea lions are different. Sea lions have small external ears. Seals have small ear openings. Sea lions get around more easily. They use front flippers to negotiate, while seals use their hind flippers. Sea lions make a lot more noise than seals. Which are you more likely to see climbing on the rocks at the zoo? Seals or sea lions?

*The tallest animals in the zoo reside at the **Hoofed Animal Complex**. Do you know what they are?*

pollution problems in our current underwater environment, stop in at "The Great Lakes: The Delicate Balance," an Academy exhibit that examines the vital ecosystem of the Great Lakes by exploring their past, present, and future. The Great Lakes, Huron, Superior, Michigan, Erie, and Ontario, hold 20 percent of the world's supply of fresh surface water.

Do you have a deep dark desire to touch creepy crawly creatures? Learn how to handle snakes and bugs or how to go spelunking through the Academy's bat caves. You can even take an overnight excursion and learn how to make a traditional Native American medicine bag and use a mono and a matate. Academy of Sciences exhibits and workshops change month to month, so call ahead to find out current schedules to avoid disappointment.

You won't be disappointed by the Academy's Gift Shop, which has a great assortment of sparkling bismuth crystals, models of fossils and dinosaurs, chemistry sets, and even a disappearing ink kit.

If you've had your fill of museum activities, visit one of Lincoln Park's twelve beaches. The best beaches for kids in this area are right north or south of Diversey Street. If you are knee deep in snow, try some cross-country skiing. To find out about cross-country ski trails, the best hills for sledding, and the cool places to ice skate, call the **Chicago Parks District** on Lincoln Park West.

Just west and a bit north of Lincoln Park in the **Lincoln Park/Depaul** area are nifty shops like **Wax Trax**, a local record shop hangout for kids, **The Children's Bookstore**, which has a small platform and stage for a story-telling hour and features the biggest selection of children's books in Chicago, and **Women and Children First**, another young reader's favorite—all on N. Lincoln.

Wanna be rowdy? Have a char-dog, boogie to the jukebox, and play a few rounds of Pop-a-Shot Basketball at **Michael's** on N. Clark, or go to **R. J. Grunts** just a few blocks away on N. Lincoln, where you can grab a bowl of chili and boogaloo to 60s Motown. If 1950 is your time zone, cruise over to **Byron's**, a real 50s-style hot dog-serving drive-in on W. North. For a look at some great films from every era, take a seat at **Facets Multimedia**, an alternative movie house on Fullerton and see old Charlie Chaplin films and children's classics like *Heidi* and *National Velvet*.

There are some gruesome gangster landmarks in this area you won't want to miss, including the site of the 1929 **St. Valentine's Day Massacre** (2122 N. Clark St.), where seven men were gunned down. Most of the victims, members of George "Bugs" Moran's gang, were shot by men masquerading as police officers. When Moran heard the news that his men were dead, he said, "Only Capone kills like that," referring to rival gangster Al Capone.

*Gangster Machine Gun Jake McGurn, hit man at the St. Valentine's Day Massacre, met **his** end while bowling at 805 N. Milwaukee (now a store). His killers left him with the following valentine: "You've lost your job, you've lost your dough, Your jewels and cars and handsome houses! Things could be worse, you know— At least you haven't lost your trousas!"*

Another famous spot is the **Biograph Theater** on N. Lincoln Avenue, where bank robber John Dillinger was ambushed by federal authorities on July 22, 1934, at 10:40 p.m. after watching a movie called *Manhattan Melodrama*. There are dents in a telephone pole near the theater. People claim these are from the bullets fired by federal agents who waited for Dillinger. They were tipped off by the criminal's girlfriend, the mysterious Lady in Red. Dillinger was shot dead on the spot.

If you're a Dead Head, you'll appreciate golfing at **Par Excellence**, an indoor miniature golf range at 1800 Clybourn Mall. Designed by a local Chicago artist, the 18th hole looks like a graveyard filled with hundreds of tiny skeletons. In the same mall, be sure to check out the spanking brand new branch of **Barbara's Bookstore** packed with bundles of books for kids.

Not far from there lies **Oz Park**, between Lincoln, Halsted, and Armitage streets. This small park is frequented by big and little kids alike. There are wooden ships, bridges, and castles to explore. The park was named for the famous story, "The Wizard of Oz," created by Chicagoans Frank Baum and W. D. Denslow. This kooky collaboration led to the invention of Dorothy, Toto, the Tin Man, the Cowardly Lion, the Scarecrow, and all those little Munchkins!

5. Cows and Rock 'n Roll (Near North, North Pier, River North)

T here are several exciting neighborhoods south of Lincoln Park and north of the Chicago River. These areas are bounded by Lake Michigan on the east and the north branch of the Chicago River on the west.

You'll hear people refer to one of Chicago's posh sections as **Magnificent Mile, Boul Mich** (short for Boulevard Michigan), or **Miracle Mile**. All the different names mean the same thing— lots of expensive stores.

Even if you don't have money to burn, you'll want to step inside **Water Tower Place** to ride in the glass elevator or cruise on escalators that can transport up to 18,000 people an hour from shop to shop. The mall has a Gap Kids and a McDonald's. F.A.O. Schwarz carries everything from giant stuffed bears to Teenage Mutant Ninja Turtles. ROCS will knock your socks off with its nifty earrings and doodads to delight. At Arcadia, pick up a wild T-shirt or a wacky neon clock that laughs.

After you've had your fill of the frivolous, walk across to the Water Tower whence the shopping area takes its name.

When the smoke settled after the Great

*A branch of Barbara's Bookstore, which has one of the greatest selections of kids' books in Chicago, is in an area called **Old Town**, a bit north and west of the Boul Mich. North and east of Boul Mich eat a bagel at **Bagel Nosh** in the **Near North** area. Above Near North and below Lincoln Park lies a wealthy residential area known as the **Gold Coast**.*

24

Chicago Fire, started on the night of October 8, 1871, two of the few buildings to survive the catastrophe were the **Water Tower Pumping Station** and the **Water Tower**, castlelike buildings built of limestone. No one is really sure how the fire began, but the most popular story is that Mrs. O'Leary's cow kicked over a lantern, setting the O'Leary barn ablaze. The flames spread out of control, and most of the city's wooden structures burned to the ground. Three hundred people were killed, and 90,000 were left homeless.

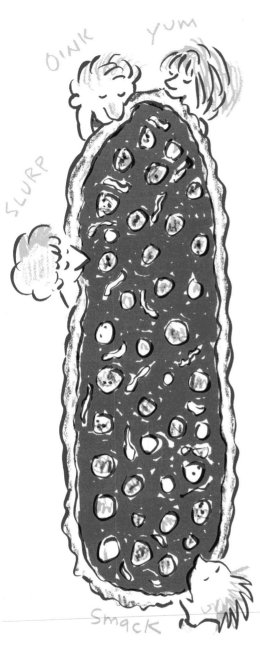

Today the Pumping Station, which is still in operation, houses a tourist attraction called **Here's Chicago**, where you can learn about the station's history. (During hot summer days, the station is capable of pumping 260 million gallons of water throughout the city of Chicago.) Here you'll also see a life-size model of **Mrs. O'Leary's cow**, a reenactment of the St. Valentine's Day Massacre, and lifelike models of detective Elliot Ness and gangster Al Capone. At the end of the tour, see a film called *City of Dreams*. The film, shot from a helicopter, lets you get a feel for Chicago from on high.

After you leave Here's Chicago, get a sky-high view of the city by visiting the world's third tallest building, the **John Hancock Center** on N. Michigan. This building resembles a humongous insect with its towering antennas. On a clear day you can see four states (Indiana, Illinois, Michigan, and Wisconsin).

The **Terra Museum of American Art** on N. Michigan has paintings by Andrew Wyeth. After you've looked at his farm scenes, take a ride in the museum's huge room-size elevator used to carry large works of art upstairs.

If you're lucky when you visit the **Museum of Contemporary Art** on E. Ontario, you might get to see some pretty wild performance artists like Vito Acconci, who used his body to create living sculpture, or you might get to see the entire building wrapped like an enormous birthday present by the artist, Christo.

Museum hopping can work up an appetite, so you may want to mosey over to **Pizzeria Uno** (or **Pizzeria Due** up the block), home of the original deep dish Chicago pizza, on E. Ohio Street, or

Pizza experts claim that Americans eat 75 acres of pizza a day.

have a slice at **Gino's** on E. Superior, then hop on
a Grand Avenue bus and head toward **North Pier**.
Here you'll find a mall packed with video arcades,
stores, and two great museums.

Whatever you do, give yourself plenty of time
to build, touch, bubble, creep, crawl, and create
your way through the fabulous, expressly-for-
kids **Express-Ways Children's Museum**. As you
enter the museum you will see the Recycle Arts
Center. For 15 cents, pick up a paper bag and fill
it full of doorknobs, wooden blocks, pieces of
cardboard, tiny bits of carpeting, little plastic
doo-hickeys that look like tiny spaceships, and
tons of other recycled industrial junk and create
something.

You can make your own Latin American folk dolls, robots, purses, money pouches, pillows—anything you can think of. From there, walk through Express-Way's Amazing Chicago and see a replica of the city with kid-sized buildings. It's a great way to get a sense of Chicago's architecture. Next, negotiate through City Hospital's wheelchair obstacle course. Step inside a model of an ambulance, take a look at real x-rays, and don't miss the Velcro heart, liver, and lungs! At the Art and Science of Bubbles Exhibit, surround yourself in huge people-sized bubbles, and at Magic and Masquerades, create West African masks, beaded jewelry, and costumes. Recycle, discover, express yourself!

For a calmer, less interactive experience, visit the **Chicago Maritime Museum**, newly reopened in 1989, and get a close look at the five-foot-long model of the *David Dowes*, a five-masted wooden schooner, and a model of the *Christopher Columbus*, a boat launched on Lake Michigan in 1893.

You can see real ships if you walk outside on North Pier. Here you can stroll, watch the boats on the lake, and get a great view of the city. In warm weather, you can walk out onto Grand Avenue and explore **Navy Pier**, built in 1916 for commercial shipping. In 1976, the city of Chicago renovated the 3,000-foot pier, making it available for a variety of uses including fairs and art exhibitions.

River North, Chicago's arty neighborhood west of Dearborn Street and a bit east of the north branch of the Chicago River, is sometimes referred to as **Suhu** (which means the area near Superior and Huron streets). Most people think "New York" when they think "modern art," but Chicago's River North is a large, vital artist community with over 50 galleries. The exhibitions here aren't geared to kids, but if the big people you are traveling with are gallery hopping, you will find plenty to see and do in the general area.

In 1991, at the Give Peace a Chance exhibit at **The Peace Museum** on W. Erie Street, you'll be able to see John Lennon's guitar and the gold record he received for his song, "Imagine." Ever wonder how to write "How you doing?" in Japanese or Russian? The Peace Post Office exhibit shows you how to translate greetings so you can write to kids in Japan and the Soviet

*At the **Dart Gallery** on W. Superior, you might still be able to smell chocolate. This building was once a candy factory. On hot days, chocolate and caramel can be seen dripping from the ceiling.*

29

Union. At the Martin Luther King, Jr., exhibit learn about the great civil rights leader's life. The exhibits here change every three months, so you may want to call first to find out what they are showing.

A bit out of the way but not too far from the River North area on W. Chicago is the ***Chicago Tribune* Freedom Center**, the plant where the *Tribune* is printed. Kids over the age of ten can take a tour and see old *Trib* headlines from the first moon landing and the day Abraham Lincoln was elected president.

If you need a rest from historical sights and museums, stop for a munchies break and a boisterous trip down rock-and-roll memory lane at **Ed Debevik's** eatery extraordinaire on N. Wells Street. The signs read "Ed's Chili Dog— The Cadillac of Chili Dogs," and waitresses are rocking to 50s tunes in their bobby socks. From there, bop on over to W. Ontario Street, where kids can, and do, hang out at the **Hard Rock Cafe** until evening hours. Here you can see Indiana Jones's leather jacket and Michael Jackson's platinum records, not to mention half of a Cadillac sticking out of the wall. Take one more step down memory lane and check out the **Rock 'n' Roll McDonald's** on N. Clark. The world's busiest, this home of the golden arches houses life-size statues of the Beatles and is open 24 hours a day. So grab a burger, sip your shake next to the 1959 Corvette parked in the window, and cool out!

6. The Loop: Pork Bellies, Cattle, and Calder (Downtown)

The **"Loop"** technically refers to the area within the loop made by elevated tracks that encircle Chicago's downtown area. The Loop also refers to the general area between Lake Michigan on the east, the Chicago River on the west and north, and Congress Parkway (some say even as far as Roosevelt Road) on the south.

You may need a couple of days to see everything in the Loop area. You'll probably want to spend at least one day exploring Chicago's inner Loop and another day downtown investigating more museums, stores, and buildings. However you decide to break it up, there are tons of great places you won't want to miss.

At the center of the Loop is the hustling, bustling financial hub of the midwestern United States. This area is also the center of government offices, some Chicago landmark buildings, and the city's great outdoor sculpture.

LaSalle Street became the city's financial center in 1865 with the building of the Board of Trade. Destroyed and rebuilt after the great Chicago Fire, the area surrounding the Board quickly grew to be a hotbed for commerce and the focus of modern architecture.

By 1837, the year Chicago officially became incorporated, there were 4,000 people living in the city, most of them in and around the area that is now known as the Loop. The Chicago metro area now has about 7 million people, many of whom work in the downtown area.

If you are a trader, you'll never see a real pork belly (the stuff that ham and bacon are made of) or a soybean. Traders speculate or guess what they think the price of a certain product will be in the future.

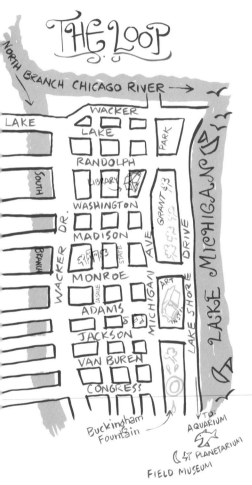

The Art Deco **Chicago Board of Trade Building** stands at the end of LaSalle, hovering above the rest of Chicago's financial district. Perched on the very top of the building is a faceless statue of **Ceres**, the Greek goddess of grain. She stands like a guardian angel over Chicago's largest and oldest futures exchange. At the **Visitor's Gallery** on the fifth floor, see how futures on things like corn, soybeans, and wheat are traded. The trading pit is the same area traders worked in almost 100 years ago. Before the use of computers, prices were written on a blackboard.

Across the street is the **Chicago Board Options Exchange**. Here you can also see what you saw at the board of trade—the "open outcry system." Translation: guys and girls dressed in funny bright-colored jackets standing around screaming and waving their arms, making and losing money.

From here, you can head up to the **Chicago Mercantile Exchange** on S. Wacker, but first take a look at the nautilus-shaped indoor fire escape at the **Rookery** on S. LaSalle Street, with its remodeled lobby by "Chicago School" architect, Frank Lloyd Wright. A plaque states this is Chicago's oldest skyscraper.

At the Merc, they are trading futures on live cattle, live hogs, pork bellies, and some financial products. The **Visitor's Gallery** on the fourth floor features an interactive video for kids explaining futures trading.

Whether you plan on stashing your cash under your pillow or investing in some soybeans, these financial centers will give you a good look at capitalism at work.

Money makes the world go around. So does

politics. At **Chicago City Hall-Cook County Building**, on Clark between Randolph and Washington, you may get to see some more shouting and arm waving if you happen by during one of Chicago's famous City Council meetings.

While Chicago may be known for LaSalle Street deals and heated political arguments in City Hall, it is also famous for its architecture. A great way to get an overview of Chicago's architectural history is to stop in at the **Archi Center** on S. Dearborn. You can sign up for a tour of architectural sights designed especially for kids called **Put Your Arms Around a Building**. This short walking tour traces the development of the skyscraper. You'll see buildings designed by Frank Lloyd Wright, Louis Sullivan, and Ludwig Mies van der Rohe, some of the most famous architects the world has ever known.

World-famous artists have also left their mark in Chicago in the form of magnificent outdoor sculpture, all within a few blocks of one another. Here are a few of them.

The Jean Dubuffet sculpture, *Monument with Standing Beast*, looks like a goofy gargoyle as it guards the entrance to the **State of Illinois Center** on Randolph Street. You can climb around on this beast and then walk inside the Star Wars-like spaceship of a building.

No Luke Skywalkers, Darth Vaders, or Han Solos in this spaceship, just somber-looking business types in blue suits. But you'll feel like you're being beamed up to the bridge when you ride the clear glass elevator all the way to the top of the building.

Just south of the Illinois Center at the **Daley**

The 24,600 glass panels in the State of Illinois Center conducted so much heat during the building's first years that people were forced to wear tropical clothes in summer to keep cool.

Center, named for the late Chicago Mayor Richard J. Daley, stands the famous rusty Picasso sculpture. It has no name other than "The Picasso." Some people say it's the head of a woman, some say it's a cow. Still others insist it's an Afghan hound. What do you think? The plaza area around the Daley Center is a popular warm weather hangout for young skateboarders from all parts of the city. In winter, bring your ice skates and carve a few figure eights. An eternal flame burns near the Picasso sculpture as a reminder of the soldiers who died fighting in the Korean and Vietnam wars.

Did you ever wonder how big the biggest base-ball bat in the world is? The biggest one in the city of Chicago is on W. Madison. The 101-foot sculpture designed by Claes Oldenburg is called *Batcolumn*. If you got all the team members

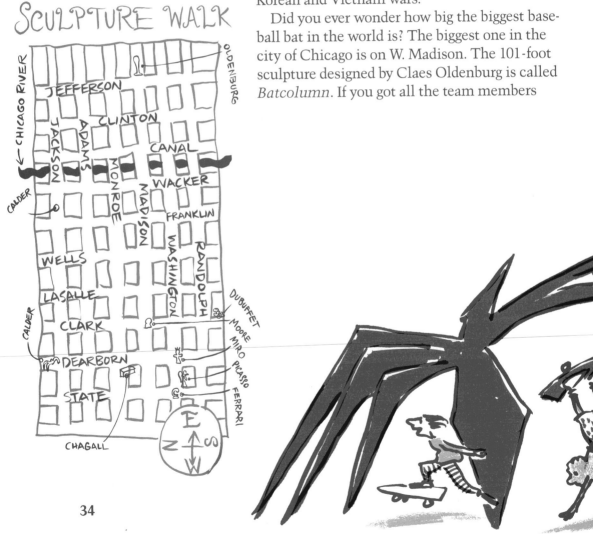

SCULPTURE WALK

CHICAGO RIVER

JEFFERSON
CLINTON
JACKSON
ADAMS
CANAL
MONROE
WACKER
MADISON
FRANKLIN
WASHINGTON
WELLS
RANDOLPH
LASALLE
CLARK
DEARBORN
STATE
CHAGALL

OLDENBURG
CALDER
CALDER
DUBUFFET
MOORE
MIRO
PICASSO
FERRARI

from the Cubs and the White Sox together, do you think they could lift this Louisville Slugger high enough to hit a home run?

People don't play baseball at the **First National Bank Plaza** on W. Monroe, but in summer little and big kids alike sit in the sun, listen to free jazz concerts, and watch street performers. This is the site of the famous mosaic, *The Four Seasons*, by Marc Chagall.

South of the Xerox building on S. Dearborn stands *Flamingo* by the artist Alexander Calder, inventor of the "mobile." This sculpture, a "stabile," may not look like a bird to you. What would you call it?

As you can see, within a few blocks you can get a good look at some of the world's most famous modern art, and you don't even have to step inside a museum.

*The Alexander Calder sculpture, **Universe**, in the entrance of the Sears Tower is the artist's largest moving mobile-like mural.*

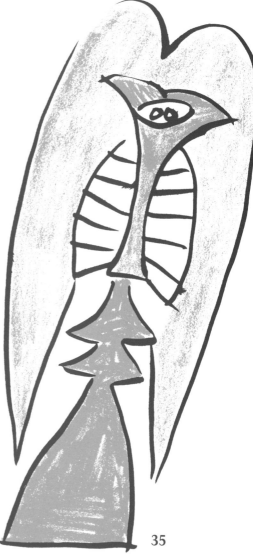

35

7. More Loop

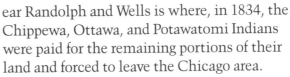

Near Randolph and Wells is where, in 1834, the Chippewa, Ottawa, and Potawatomi Indians were paid for the remaining portions of their land and forced to leave the Chicago area.

Another historic spot is at 100 W. Monroe Street, where there is a cow path that was reserved for farmer Willard Jones's cow. A 1938 city ordinance states cows are to be allowed to walk through the Loop between 7 a.m. and 7 p.m. There aren't many cows grazing through Chicago these days, but if you plan to bring a bovine buddy with you when you visit, you'll know where to take it.

In 1899, architect Louis Sullivan designed the Schlesinger and Mayer store, which is now called the **Carson Pirie Scott and Company Building** on S. State Street. Make sure to take a look at the rounded windows and delicately detailed iron-work above the entrance to the building. This is a prize example of what's known as "Chicago School of Architecture" at its most ornamental stage.

Another famous department store is **Marshall Field's** on N. State Street, which sells "famous"

Frango Mints, the best chocolate in the world. For generations, people have shopped here and used the huge outdoor clock as a meeting place. But when you look, you'll see two clocks. In Chicago, if someone says, "I'll meet you under the Marshall Field's clock," it means the one near Randolph, not the one near Washington. Be sure to go inside to the Crystal Palace, an old-fashioned ice cream parlor, and have a squiggly sundae with gummy spiders, worms, and insects. If you're bugged by bugs, you can also order a plain scoop.

In the old days, a scoop or two might have been what you'd have after an afternoon of comedy at the old **Chicago Theater** on N. State, where the Marx Brothers, Bob Hope, and Jerry Lewis all performed. The theater, built in 1921, was almost demolished in 1982, but Chicagoans put up a fuss. It was restored, and now you may be able to catch an ice show, a magic show, or a musical extravaganza.

If you want a break from all the historic spots, take a walk over to the **City of Chicago Store** on W. Randolph Street. This is a good place to pick up Chicago posters, sweatshirts, books on the city, or a Lincoln Park Zoo belt buckle. Or how about a T-shirt with a picture of Chicago's "L" system and the words, "I had a 'L' of a time in Chicago."

For comic relief, head to **Comic Relief** on E. Madison, a small friendly store with new and used comic books. Some rare comics sell for up to $30,000.00. This store doesn't carry anything that pricey. But they do have a big selection of new and used Batman and Spiderman comics and lots of X-Men titles.

*Whether you hear a concert in the park, see a puppet show at **Hystopolis Puppet Theater**, kick up your heels and sing along with a musical production at **ETA Creative Arts Foundation**, or visit **Second City's Children's Theater**, you'll want to check for dates and locations of specific performances. Pick up a copy of the* Chicago Reader, *a free weekly paper,* Chicago Magazine, *or the* Sunday Chicago Tribune *and check for children's listings.*

The largest hand-launched kite ever flown in Grant Park was 83 feet long. Chicago is a great place to fly kites. It really is the Windy City.

You can take your comic books and read them over at the **Chicago Public Library Cultural Center** on E. Washington. The building, a historic landmark, will stay the same, but the library itself, including the children's library, called the **Thomas Hughes Room**, will be moving sometime in fall 1991 to a brand-new building. It will be called the **Harold Washington Public Library**, named for the late mayor. The library offers all kinds of special programs including puppet shows, mimes, jugglers, and musicians. There have even been special workshops on pet care and proper manners!

Proper manners are essential when attending a Chicago Symphony Orchestra concert at **Orchestra Hall** on S. Michigan; no fidgeting, whispering, or running around here.

But if you don't feel like behaving yourself, go make some noise in **Grant Park**. In summer, fly a kite, play baseball, and visit Buckingham Fountain, where you can see a nighttime light show or listen to music during the world-famous Gospel, Blues, and Jazz Fests. During July, you won't want to miss Taste of Chicago, the city's biggest food festival offering thousands of sumptuous samplings. The James C. Petrillo Music Shell hosts the Grant Park Concert Series.

Whether you're listening to a concert, batting a ball, or passing the pigskin, remember to say hello to Abraham Lincoln. A statue of the Illinois-born president stands in between Buckingham Fountain and the **Art Institute** on S. Michigan, a museum packed with statues and Seurat's famous *A Sunday Afternoon on the Island of La Grande Jatte*, a huge painting made up entirely of dots.

But you don't have to tromp through the entire museum to see great artwork. The Art Institute designed a kid-size museum called the **Junior Museum**. You can paint there, or bring a sack lunch to the picnic room and take a break. You might get to see someone like Lamanidi Fakeye, a fifth-generation Yoruba wood carver from Nigeria, as he demonstrates African wood carving techniques.

The Junior Museum also features special programs throughout the year. You can learn how to make Japanese fans or help paint huge murals.

In the **Art Institute Little Library**, find out how to be a regular Sherlock Holmes by playing "I Spy," a game that will have you running all over the museum discovering the answers to mysterious clues.

Chicago-style blues music was born in the 1930s when many musicians from the South came to the Windy City and began adding new guitar techniques to traditional blues music. Chicago Blues had its heyday in the 1950s. Some Chicago Blues greats: Muddy Waters, James Cotton, and Buddy Guy.

And, of course, on your way in or out, don't forget to say hello to two of Chicago's most beloved animals, the bronze lions that guard the entrance to the Art Institute. In 1986, the Chicago Bears won the Super Bowl. After the game fans adorned the famous felines with football helmets.

The **Maurice Spertus Museum of Judaica**, just south of the Art Institute on S. Michigan, has a permanent, hands-on exhibit of Near Eastern archaeology for kids called the Artifact Center.

Walk a bit south and west and you'll find the **Museum of Broadcast Communications** on S. Wells, where you and a partner can have 15 minutes of fame in front of the camera reading the teleprompter, reporting the news, and giving sports scores as anchors of your own news show. You can spend hours reviewing tapes of the TV shows your parents used to watch, like "Dobie Gillis," "Lost in Space," and "The Flintstones."

8. Mollies, Mummies, and Moon Rocks (South of the Loop)

It's easy to forget, but mummies are people too. An often asked question is, "What are mummies made of?" Mummies are dead people or animals that have been preserved.

Chicago is famous for its **Field Museum of Natural History** on S. Lake Shore Drive which owns about 19,000,000 bones, stones, and all kinds of artifacts. Originally opened in 1894, it has over nine acres of exhibits to see, touch, hear, feel, and investigate.

But as one Chicago kid warns, "The Field Museum is very, very big, very hot, and you can get very tired in there!" It's true. It is big and hot, and you can get tired in there, but for goodness sake, don't let that stop you. An important piece of advice for you and any adults you may be kidding around with: Don't try to see or do too much. A good idea is to visit this museum and focus on one or two sections. When you get tired, go outside and play frisbee.

Some Chicago kid favorites at the Field Museum are the Sizes Exhibit, the Skeleton and Reptile Hall, Dinosaur Hall, the Traveling Pacific Exhibit, and the Inside Ancient Egypt Exhibit. At the Sizes Exhibit on the first floor, try on the biggest pair of blue jeans ever made. These giant-sized overalls are big enough for at least two whole regular-sized kids. There is a table and chair that will remind big kids of what it felt

WHAT'S A MUMMY'S FAVORITE MUSIC?

RAP!

LU NU

Jr. scientists: Recheck facts. New discoveries are made all the time and even experts make mistakes.

like to be three years old, and there is also the optical illusion room that will make you shrink and grow like magic!

In the Skeleton and Reptile Hall on the first floor, there are backbones, leg bones, jawbones, and craniums. Don't miss the 45-foot whale skeleton hanging from the ceiling. How many Jonahs do you think this whale could've swallowed?

At the south end of Stanley Field Hall on the first floor sits a 6½-foot-long, 100-million-year-old thigh bone of a brachiosaurus. This dynamo of a dinosaur weighed in at more than 85.63 tons. He apparently had a tiny mouth and lots of bad teeth. The 72-foot *Apatosaurus* skeleton, on the second floor, could definitely use some dental work.

To see what peoples of the Pacific ate, walk through a turn-of-the-century New Guinea village at one of the museum's newest features, the Traveling the Pacific Exhibit on the second floor. You can sit in the Spirit Canoe and test your navigational skills with the Seafaring Survival computer game. With only the stars, meager provisions, and crew, will you be able to master the high seas?

You won't need a caravan of camels to climb 35 feet down into the reconstructed 4,000-year-old tomb of Unis-ankh, the son of an ancient pharaoh. The Inside Ancient Egypt Exhibit has 23 real mummies. The mummy of Harwa, found in the Egyptian city of Karnak, looks pretty good for being almost 3,000 years old!

To avoid total exhaustion, make a pit stop at the **McDonald's** or the **Snack Bar**, both in the museum's basement, before you head over to the Shedd Aquarium.

You'll want to get to the **John G. Shedd Aquarium** before the sharks, sea turtles, and moray eels get their morning or afternoon meal at 11:00 a.m. and 2:00 p.m. A diver, equipped with a special microphone, can answer questions while diving into the 90,000-gallon tank to feed all of the 500 tropical fish. The sharks go crazy, the moray eels sometimes nibble at the diver's heels, and the sea turtles get downright snappy.

In fall 1990, the world's largest indoor aquarium opens its new saltwater oceanarium, which will re-create a natural habitat for sea otters, provide a 400,000-gallon pool for beluga whales, and house a two-million-gallon pool that will be home to white-sided dolphins and Pacific blue whales. There has been quite a controversy over the opening of the oceanarium. Many people think it's cruel to keep large sea mammals in captivity. What do you think?

East of the aquarium sits the **Adler Planetarium**, where if you look west, you'll get a spectacular view of the Chicago skyline. Your exposure to the universe starts with a zippy multimedia show in the Universe Theater which includes several films and slides projected onto the ceiling and walls. From there, be launched toward the heavens in the Sky Theater where you will see how the stars and planets move across the sky.

After the show, travel to the space transporters and beam yourself up to Venus in the **Hall of Space Exploration**. Step into specially designed booths that show you the difference between your body weight on Earth and your weight on other planets in the solar system.

Don't miss the sharp space suit worn by U.S. astronauts and the 4-billion-year-old moon rock

The Shedd Aquarium is the only place outside of the West Coast where you can see Alaskan sea otter pups that were saved after the 1989 Exxon Valdez oil spill.

Feeling pretty skinny? Wait 'til you get to Jupiter. If you weigh 96 lbs. on Earth, you'd weigh 235 lbs. on Jupiter.

picked up by David Scott, one of the astronauts aboard the Apollo 15 mission.

In the gift shop, you can find space patches, gemstone rings, astronomy capsules, and a prism scope. If you're hungry, have some astronaut food or head out to **Burnham Park** for a picnic.

Meigs Field, across from Burnham Park, is a private airstrip, and from time to time daredevil flyers, the Blue Angels, leave their trail across the sky. Directly across from Meigs Field is **Soldier Field**, where the Chicago Bears put on a show of their own during football season.

Just southwest of Meigs, you may want to stop in at **McCormick Place**, the largest exhibition hall in America. There might be a boat show, car show, or the National Gin Rummy Tournament.

North and west of McCormick Place in the **Prairie Avenue Historic District** is the **Glessner House**, built in 1887, and the **Widow Clarke House**, the oldest house in the city of Chicago and one of the few homes to survive the great Chicago Fire.

Some historic Chicago gangster moments are recorded at the **American Police Center and Museum** at its new location, just northwest of the Prairie Avenue district on S. State Street. The museum's Gangster Alley has photographs of such notorious types as Al Capone, a model of a real jail cell, and an electric chair. There is also a display of hundreds of police shields and badges.

9. Science, Sojourner, and the South Side

The **Hyde Park/Kenwood** area of Chicago is only a few miles by car, bus, or train from the Prairie Avenue District, the Field Museum, or McCormick Place.

This south side section of the city is home to the switch flippingest, button pushingest, handle turningest, lever liftingest museum in the world. Not to mention home to one of Chicago's most successfully racially integrated neighborhoods, the world's first controlled self-sustaining chain reaction, and one of the world's most prestigious universities.

The **Museum of Science and Industry**, located in **Jackson Park**, was originally built as part of a world's fair called the World's Columbian Exposition of 1893. The museum officially opened in 1933 and is visited by more than four million people a year. Like the Field Museum, the Museum of Science and Industry is gigantic, so don't expect to see everything in one visit.

Some must-sees are the real German submarine, the U-505 captured during World War II (you can see Lake Michigan from the boat's periscope), and the coal mine, where you'll drop down 50 feet into what seems to be the real

Love to know what's going on inside your left ventricle? Take a hike through the 16-foot model of the human heart.

thing. Near the coal mine exit is Colleen Moore's Fairy Castle Doll House, complete with solid gold dishes, a "bear skin" rug with teeth from a mouse, and the world's smallest Bible, printed in 1840.

At the Henry Crown Space Center, slip into some 3-D shades and blast off in the simulated space shuttle ride. You'll forget you are in the museum, in the city of Chicago, and even on the planet Earth.

Make sure you step into the OmniMax Theater and hold onto your seat while you watch films like *To Fly*, a movie that lets you feel what it's actually like to fly. You might also want to hold onto your stomach for this one.

If you lost your appetite, you'll get it back again after visiting the Food for Life Exhibit, complete with scrumptious displays of fake food, a fitness center, and an incubator full of hatching chickens. You'll find out what all those milk shakes and french fries are doing to you.

If you're ready for a salad, try the Century Room, or if you still have a hankering for hot dogs, try the Main Street Cafe, or how about, "I scream, you scream, we all scream for ice cream," which is what you'll scream at Finnegan's Ice Cream Parlor.

Not far from the museum at the **University of Chicago** campus stands the **Robie House**, designed by Frank Lloyd Wright and considered one of the most outstanding American homes built in the twentieth century.

Still mad for mummies? Walk one block west of the Robie House and you'll find the **Oriental Institute**, where at the back of the first big hall you'll find several mummies, a huge sculpture of King Tut, and scary skeletons.

These skeletons aren't half as scary as *Nuclear Energy*, Henry Moore's 12-ton sculpture commemorating the site where man first harnessed nuclear energy. The first self-sustained nuclear chain reaction took place on December 2, 1942,

Sojourner Truth, a great black woman orator who lived from 1797 to 1883 said, "When I left bondage I left everything behind. I went to the Lord and asked him for a new name. Lord gave me Sojourner."

at 3:25 p.m. under what used to be the Stagg Field Grandstands and is now a library.

Just west of here is the **Du Sable Museum of African American History** on E. 56th Place where you can find out about the lives of famous African Americans like Frederick Douglass, Sojourner Truth, Malcolm X, and Martin Luther King, Jr. The museum has special workshops for children on topics like African mask making, the Kwanza celebration, and the Haitian carnival. The multimedia center has a library full of films and jazz recordings. The gift shop offers books on black theater, maps of Africa, and coloring books.

The Du Sable Museum sits in **Washington Park**, a great place for sledding in the winter and picnicking in the summer.

If you didn't bring your lunch and you didn't eat at the Museum of Science and Industry, try a famous Chicago pan or stuffed pizza at **Edwardo's** on E. 57th Street or have a bowl of chili on E. 53rd Street at **Mellow Yellow**, a winner in Chicago's Taste Fest. If you yearn for tofu and nori, then stop in at the **Sunflower Seed Health Food Store** at Harper Court. Next door, find toys galore at **Toys Et Cetera**. For a good read, hit **Powell's** on E. 57th and Harper. **57th Street Books** on E. 57th and Kimbark has one of the biggest children's sections in the city. In between chapters catch a cup of hot chocolate at the **Medici Gallery and Coffee House** on E. 57th.

By now, you might think you've seen all there is to see in Chicago, but you've only just begun. Did you know Chicago is made up of more than 75 neighborhoods? You'll never be able to see them all in one visit, but the next chapter covers some of the highlights that shouldn't be missed.

10. Fortune Cookies and Fried Eel (Ethnic Neighborhoods)

The Chinese believe that a doorway or a gate painted red brings good luck, health, and happiness.

From the days of Du Sable, people from around the globe have come to make a life for themselves in Chicago. People from Ireland, Germany, Poland, Italy, Greece, Lithuania, China, Vietnam, Africa, Mexico, and everywhere else you can think of have settled in Chicago's neighborhoods. The ethnic populations of these areas continue to grow and change from generation to generation. Some of these neighborhoods are within walking distance of the downtown area; most are a bus, car, or "L" ride away. Give yourself plenty of time to sightsee. Don't try to visit Rogers Park and Pilsen in the same day. But if you want to try dim sum, or see intricately colored Easter eggs, or buy silks from India, get ready to explore some more.

Did you ever see a Chinese telephone booth? Or how about street signs and shop signs written in Chinese? As you enter **Chinatown** (just a couple of miles south of the Loop), make sure you walk through the Gate of Happiness for good luck.

Tins of teas, jade Buddhas, dried seaweed, plum candy, Chinese/English calculators, Chinese hats, and Crazy Mix line the shelves at the

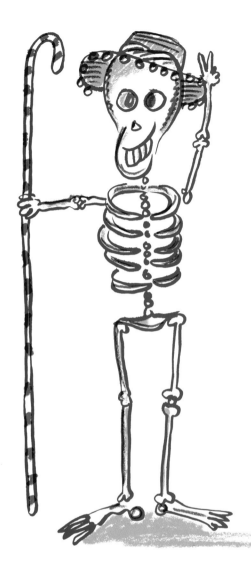

Día de los Muertos means "Day of the Dead." It is a day on which Mexican people honor their dead relatives with song, dance, food, and festivities. They believe dead folks appreciate the hullabaloo.

Mee Wah Company on S. Wentworth. You'll really go crazy in **Bang, Bang**, a store filled with Chinese yoyos, flutes, clothes for kids, and a whole assortment of toys from China. The **Happy Garden Bakery** sells mountains of fortune cookies as well as other Chinese baked goods.

A visit to Chinatown is not complete without a Chinese meal. There are several restaurants from which to choose. The most popular is **Three Happiness** on W. Cermak. A good alternative if the Three Happiness is too crowded is the **Chiam Restaurant** on S. Wentworth, where you can try everything from dynamite dim sum to moo shu pork.

Burritos are the Mexican version of moo shu. Instead of a thin pancake wrapped around shredded vegetables and pork, this is a flour tortilla hugging a bunch of beans or any combination of beans, chili, cheese, and meat. While walking through **Pilsen** (on the Near Southwest Side), formerly a Czechoslovakian area, now Chicago's mostly Mexican neighborhood, notice the smell of tortillas filling the air. On the streets, kids kick soccer balls and call out to each other in Spanish.

The **Mexican Fine Arts Center Museum** holds the largest Día de los Muertos celebration in the country. So if you're there during the festivities (October 9 through November 29), dance, sing, and party down! Try a taco, burrito, or an enchilada at **Nuevo Leon** on W. 18th, one of Pilsen's best Mexican restaurants. The food's great and inexpensive.

A historically important area is the **Near West Side**. Jane Addams moved into this overcrowded and poor neighborhood in 1889 and started **Hull**

House on S. Halsted Street, a settlement house with public baths (many people couldn't afford to have private showers), playgrounds, a theater, a kitchen, and other facilities for the area's poor. Two of the settlement's original buildings remain. These buildings were turned into a museum where you can see Jane Addams's office, maps of the settlement, and a photograph of Addams herself.

A few blocks south you'll find the **Maxwell Street Market** (at Halsted and 14th sts.), the city's biggest flea market where you can find absolutely anything from blenders to blintzes and pork chop sandwiches. Here on Sunday mornings, you can hear real Chicago Blues bands playing on street corners for free. Musicians often sell cassettes of their music.

North of there at Randolph and Desplaines streets sits **Haymarket Square**, scene of the 1886 worker's riot, where a bomb exploded and killed several policemen and civilians.

This area is more peaceful now and is home to some good Jewish, Greek, and Italian restaurants. Try a corned beef sandwich at **Manny's Coffee Shop** on S. Jefferson or some pizza at **Gennaro's** on Taylor. Or at the **Parthenon** on S. Halsted, try saganaki, a flaming cheese dish. As the waiter serves the saganaki and douses the flames with a squirt of lemon juice, you and your friends can shout "Opa!" Another place for great Greek cuisine is the **Greek Islands**, just off S. Halsted.

Want something sweet? Try some incredibly edibly scrumptious sticky buns at **Ann Sathers** on N. Clark in **Andersonville** (on the North Side), Chicago's Swedish neighborhood. The

*If sports are your sport, you already know Chicago is famous for more than just baseball and football. The **Chicago Black Hawks**, who take their name from the famous Indian chief, not the birds, whack that little puck around from mid-October to mid-April at the Chicago Stadium. Another beloved bunch of Chicago animals are the **Chicago Bulls**. Michael "Air" Jordan and the rest of the team slam dunk their way through basketball season at the same stadium.*

Swedish Museum, also on N. Clark, has a listing of special events for kids that include basket-making and Swedish harvest celebrations.

Looking for a traditional Vietnamese celebration, complete with a dragon dance, music, and outdoor lanterns? During the Chinese New Year, which usually takes place sometime in January or February and lasts about 15 days, visit Chicago's **New Chinatown** (south of Andersonville), home to many Vietnamese immigrants. At the Viet Hoa Market, see live crabs, squid, and huge eels.

South of here catch a fly ball at **Wrigleyville's** famous home of the Chicago Cubs, **Wrigley Field**. These baby bears are loved by their fans. Near Wrigley Field, bat your own balls in the batting cages at **Sluggers**, a game room with over 40 sport-related activities.

If eel makes you squeal, grab a hot dog at

Fluky's in **Rogers Park**, Chicago's northernmost neighborhood, where they give kids things like bubble gum in the shape of hot dogs and moon monster rings. The **Rogers Park Community Arts Center** has activities and a puppet theater for kids. The markets on Devon Avenue are filled with all kinds of East Indian items, everything from spices to silk saris. Try some curried chicken, basmati rice, and alou gohbi. Remember, Indian food is spicy. Cool off with a magical mango shake at the **Gandhi India Restaurant**.

For some real magic, check out **Magic, Inc.** on N. Lincoln in the area called **Ravenswood** or **Lincoln Square** (on the Northwest Side). Let Bruce, the resident magician, pull some coins or maybe a flower out of your ear.

Two museums off the beaten track (on the Near Northwest Side) which shouldn't be missed

The National Hot Dog and Sausage Council says that 80 percent of all people who go to baseball games eat hot dogs.

if you're cruising nearby are the **Polish Museum** on N. Milwaukee, full of model ships and painted Easter eggs, and the **Ukrainian National Museum** on W. Chicago Avenue, where you'll see more intricately painted eggs and hear stories of ancient Ukrainian culture.

Another-out-of-the-way museum but one worth visiting on the Near West Side is the **Museum of Holography** on W. Washington, where you'll say to yourself, "No, that can't be a real cat inside that picture." You won't believe your eyes as you marvel at two-dimensional pictures that appear as three-dimensional objects.

The Lithuanian village and the medieval room at the **Balzekas Museum of Lithuanian Culture** are designed with children in mind. This museum in **West Lawn**, on the Southwest Side, has a replica of an old Lithuanian village, armor, and puppet shows.

Chicago has the biggest Polish population outside of Warsaw, Poland, as well as the biggest Lithuanian population outside of Lithuania.

11. The Outer Limits (Chicago's Suburbs)

C hicago has still more in store for you. To see some Midwest hot spots, you'll have to venture far and wide outside the city limits to some of Chicago's great suburban sights. You will need to travel by train, car, or bus. The following places are in Chicago's north and west suburbs.

Ever want to see yourself as a glamour girl in a glittering golden gown, high heels, and pearls? Or chief of a famous hospital? Or maybe an airline pilot? At the **Kohl Children's Museum** in Wilmette (one of Chicago's North Shore suburbs), dress up and be a star in your own videotaped TV show.

Wear crazy face paints, float inside your own kid-sized soap bubble at the Human Bubble Exhibit, and shop at a miniature grocery store, but don't try to eat the food—it's all fake! Kohl's mini Jewel/Osco food market is an exact kid-sized replica of a real supermarket.

Race through the pages of the book, *Where's Waldo?* in a new traveling exhibit that will keep you searching for the crazy capped cad. Meet a real-life Waldo and get his autograph.

At Kohl's Learning Store, you'll find a great assortment of dinosaur books, crystal-growing

*Getting ready to leave Chicago? If you are flying, consider a tour of **O'Hare Airport**, the busiest airport in the world. If your plane departs from **Midway**, you'll take off from an airport that sits right in the middle of the city. Traveling by train? Look around **Union Station**, just west of the Sears Tower and see where the movie,* The Untouchables, *was filmed.*

sets, rocket ships, and doll-making kits.

From here, feast on fabulous flapjacks at the nearby **Original Pancake House** on Green Bay Road. This well-known Chicago area landmark also serves hefty hamburgers, sandwiches, gyros, and delicious desserts.

Not far from here is the famous **Bahai House of Worship**, which looks like a huge orange juice squeezer and is definitely worth a peek if you are on your way to an outdoor summer concert at the **Ravinia Festival** (north of Wilmette) in the Chicago suburb of Highland Park. Ravinia's season runs from May through September and offers all kinds of concerts featuring everything from the Chicago Symphony to dance companies and special young people's music programs.

Buildings, concrete, buses, trains, noise, and people can be exhausting. If the city scene's got you screaming for trees and trails, take a hike through the **Morton Arboretum** (in Lisle, a town west of Chicago), sniff some snapdragons at the **Chicago Botanic Garden** in Glencoe (just north of the city and south of Ravinia), or walk through the wilds of **Brookfield Zoo** (west of the city), where you can see a dolphin show. **Oak Park** is not far from the zoo and is due west of downtown Chicago. Here you can visit Frank Lloyd Wright's home and studio.

12. Wave Good-bye to the Windy City

ow that you've been to the top of the world, ridden the L, eaten dim sum, heard the blues, bought T-shirts and postcards, cruised the river and the lake, traveled in space, batted a ball or two, and maybe even flown a kite in one of the Windy City's windiest parks, it's time to move on.

Surely, your trip has been a breeze, but even if you got on the wrong train or didn't like the taste of grilled eel, you probably realize you've learned oodles of new things.

Traveling is the greatest way to try exotic foods, hear foreign languages, understand different cultures, and even make new friends.

Maybe you've kept a written log of your adventures, taken photographs, or even drawn some pictures. However you've chosen to preserve your multitude of memories, you've had tons of fun. Don't worry if you didn't get to see everything; remember, you can always come back to that great, second to none, midwestern metropolis, your kind of town—Chicago!

Events in the Windy City

January
Cubs Fan Convention
  Wrigley Field
  312-951-CUBS
University of Chicago Folk Festival
  312-702-9793

February
Azalea and Camellia Show
  Lincoln Park and Garfield Park Conservatories
  312-294-2493
Black History Month
  Chicago Public Library Cultural Center and
  the Du Sable Museum of African American
  History
  312-346-3278
Chicago Auto Show
  McCormick Place
  312-698-6630
Chinese New Year Parade
  Wentworth Avenue and Cermak Road
  312-326-5607

March
Lithuanian Easter Egg Decorating Workshops
and Display
  312-582-6500
Maple Syrup Festival
  312-583-8970
Medinah Shrine Circus
  Crippled Children's Hospital
  312-266-5000
St. Patrick's Day Parade
  The Loop
  312-744-4691

April
Brookfield Zoo Easter Parade and Bonnet Contest
  312-242-2630
Chicago Cubs opening day
  Wrigley Field
  312-878-2827
Chicago Latino Film Festival
  312-327-3184
Chicago White Sox opening day
  Comiskey Park
  312-559-1212
International Theater Festival of Chicago
  312-664-3370
Spring and Easter Flower Show
  Lincoln Park and Garfield Park Conservatories
  312-294-2493

May
Buckingham Fountain Display
  Grant Park at Congress and Lake Shore Dr.
Chicago International Art
Exposition
  Navy Pier
  312-787-6858
Chicago International Festival
of Flowers and Gardens
  312-787-6858
Greek Independence Day Parade
  312-787-6858
Polish Constitution Day Parade
  312-286-0500
Walk with Israel
  312-675-2200

June

57th Street Art Fair
   the block bounded by 56th and 57th Streets
   and Kenwood and Kimbark Avenues
Body Politic Street Festival
   312-871-3000 or 348-7901
Brandeis University Used Book Sale
   312-446-6177
Chicago Blues Festival
   Petrillo Music Shell
   312-744-3315
Chicago Book and Memorabilia Fair
   Dearborn Street
   312-663-1595
Chicago Gospel Festival
   Petrillo Music Shell
   312-744-3315
Latino Film Festival
   Getz Theater of Columbia College
   312-327-3184
Old Town Art Fair
   312-337-5962

July

Air and Water Show
   North Avenue Beach
   312-294-2494
Fourth of July Celebrations
   Grant Park
   312-294-2420
Greek Festival
   St. Andrew's Greek Orthodox Church
   312-334-4515
Howard Street Alive!
   312-508-5885
Neighborhood festivals
   Mayor's Office of Special Events
   312-744-3315
Sheffield Garden Walk and Festival
   312-327-4148
Taste of Chicago
   Grant Park
   312-744-3315
Taste of Lincoln Avenue
   312-472-9046

August

Broadway Art Fair
   312-248-8285

Chicago Jazz Festival
   Petrillo Music Shell
   312-744-3135
Chicago RiverFest
   312-922-4020
Medieval Fair in Oz Park
   312-880-5200
Venetian Night
   Monroe Street Harbor to the Planetarium
   312-294-2200
   312-744-3315

September

Chicago International Folk Fair
   312-744-3315
Chicago International New Art Forms Exposition
   Navy Pier
   312-787-6858
Mexican Independence Day Parade
   The Loop
   312-674-5838

October
Chicago International Antiques Show
  Navy Pier
  312-787-6858
Chicago International Film Festival
  312-644-3400
Columbus Day Parade
  312-372-6788
Dinosaur Days
  Field Museum
  312-922-9410
Morton Arboretum Bonsai Society Show
  312-968-0074
Multimedia's Chicago International
Festival of Children's Films
  312-281-9075
Ringling Bros. & Barnum & Bailey Circus
  Chicago Stadium
  312-733-5300

November
Arts Expressions
  312-895-5300
Christmas Around the World
  Museum of Science and Industry
  312-684-1414
Christmas Tree Lighting

  Daley Center Plaza
Chrysanthemum Show
  Garfield Park and Lincoln Park Conservatories
  312-533-1281
Lithuanian Christmas Straw Ornament
Workshops
  Balzekas Museum of Lithuanian Culture
  312-582-6500
Veterans Day Parade
  312-744-3515

December
A Christmas Carol
  Goodman Theater
  312-443-3800
Brookfield Zoo's Christmas Party
  Children's Zoo
  312-242-2630
Christmas Flower Show
  Lincoln Park and Garfield Park Conservatories
  312-294-2493
In the Spirit
  Chicago Public Library Cultural Center
  312-346-3278
Nutcracker Ballet
  Arie Crown Theater
  312-791-6000

Appendix

Adler Planetarium
1300 S. Lake Shore Dr.
312-322-0300
Handicapped Access

**American Police Center &
Museum**
1705-25 S. State St.
312-431-0005

Archi Center
330 S. Dearborn
312-782-1776

Art Institute of Chicago
410 S. Michigan Ave.
312-443-3600
Children's tours 312-443-3688
Handicapped Access

**Balzekas Museum
of Lithuanian Culture**
6500 S. Pulaski Rd.
312-582-6500

Bicycle Chicago Rental
804 W. Randolph
312-738-9754

Brookfield Zoo
8400 W. 31st
Brookfield
312-242-2630

Bureau of Traffic
Engineering and Operations
320 N. Clark St.,Rm. 402
312-744-4684

**Chicago Academy of
Sciences**
2001 N. Clark St.
312-871-2668

**Chicago Architecture
Foundation**
1800 S. Prairie Ave.
312-326-1393

Chicago Board of Trade
LaSalle at Jackson
312-435-3625
or 312-435-3590

**Chicago Board Options
Exchange**
400 S. LaSalle
312-786-5600

Chicago Botanic Garden
Lake Cook Rd.
Glencoe
708-835-5440

**Chicago City Hall Cook
County Bldg.**
121 North LaSalle
312-744-5000

Chicago Historical Society
1601 N. Clark St.
312-642-4600
Handicapped Access

Chicago Maritime Museum
455 E. Illinois St.
312-836-4343

Chicago Mercantile Exchange
30 S. Wacker Dr.
312-930-1000

Chicago Park District
425 McFetridge Dr.
312-294-2200

Chicago Public Library
Cultural Center
78 E. Washington St.
312-269-2900

Chicago Stadium
(Bulls & Black Hawks)
1800 W. Madison
312-733-5300

Chicago Symphony Orchestra
220 S. Michigan
312-435-6666

Chicago Tourism Council
163 E. Pearson St.
312-280-5740

Chicago Tribune's Freedom Center
777 W. Chicago Ave.
312-222-3232

Children's Theater of Second City
1616 Wells St.
312-337-3992

City of Chicago
Department of Water
Tours, call 312-744-7001

City of Chicago Store
174 W. Randolph St.
312-332-0055

Comiskey Park
(White Sox)
324 W. 35th St.
312-924-1000

CTA Bus Information
W. Merchandise Mart Plaza
312-664-7200

Du Sable Museum of African History
740 E. 56 Place
312-947-0600
Handicapped Access

Express-Ways Children's Museum
435 E. Illinois St.
312-527-1000
Handicapped Access

Field Museum of Natural History
S. Lake Shore Dr. at
E. Roosevelt Rd.
312-922-9410
Handicapped Access

Francis Parker Recycling Center
N. Clark & Webster
312-549-0172

Glessner House
1800 S. Prairie
312-326-1393

Grant Park
  Soldier Field Stadium
  16th St. & the Lake
  312-294-2200
  Abraham Lincoln Monument
  Congress Dr. between
  Michigan Ave. & Columbus Dr.

Grant Park Concerts
James C. Petrillo Music Shell
E. Jackson & Columbus Dr.
312-294-2420

John Hancock Center Observatory
875 N. Michigan Ave.
312-751-3681

Here's Chicago
163 E. Pearson
312-467-7114

Hull House
800 S. Halsted
312-413-5353

Hystopolis Puppet Theatre
Free Street Community Arts
Center
441 W. North Blvd.
312-787-7387

Illinois State Tourist Information Center
310 S. Michigan Ave.
312-793-2094

Kohl Children's Museum
165 Green Bay Road
Wilmette
708-251-7781 or 708-256-6056

Lincoln Park
2045 Lincoln Park West
312-294-4750
  Conservatory
  Fullerton & Stockton Dr.
  312-294-4770
  Farm-in-the-Zoo
  312-294-4662
  Theater on the Lake
  Fullerton & Lake Shore Dr.
  312-348-7075

Lincoln Park Bike Rental
312-294-4684

Lincoln Park Paddleboat Rental
312-871-3999

Lincoln Park Zoo General Information
2200 N. Cannon Dr.
312-294-4660

McCormick Place
McCormick Pl. &
Lake Shore Dr.
312-791-7500

Mexican Fine Arts Center Museum
1852 W. 19th St.
312-738-1503

Morton Arboretum
Lisle
708-968-0074

Museum of Broadcast Communications
800 S. Wells St.
312-987-1500
Handicapped Access